BIRDS

of Britain
and Northern Europe

Credits

Netscribes Inc.,

Created by Netscribes
www.netscribes.com

Production Head Ravi Lakhina
Art Director Dibakar Acharjee
Senior Designer Shilpi Sarkar
Author Binita Roy
Editor Anand Mani
Art Editor Shrey Bhal

Copyright: North Parade Publishing Ltd.
4 North Parade, Bath, BA1 1LF, UK

First Published: 2010

ISBN - 0-7554-8753-2
Printed in China

Picture Credits

Contents

Introduction

Birds...we see them everywhere, flitting about, perching on trees and wires, singing their songs. Birds are an amazing and diverse group of animals. Colourful, sweet-voiced and sometimes quite playful, they are best known for their ability to fly: albatrosses glide long distances over the open sea where there is no place to land and rest; hummingbirds hover motionless in mid-air as they suck the nectar from flowers; and eagles swoop down to capture prey with pinpoint accuracy.

What makes them birds?

Does that mean that all birds can fly? No. It is the possession of feathers that identifies them as birds, not their ability to fly. Did you know that birds are the only animals in the world with feathers? All birds have feathers, but not all of them can fly. In fact, some species such as kiwis and penguins lost their ability to fly long ago. They decided to live either completely on land or else use their wings for swimming.

Where did they come from?

Birds evolved from reptiles in the Jurassic Period – that is between 199.6 and 145.5 million years ago.

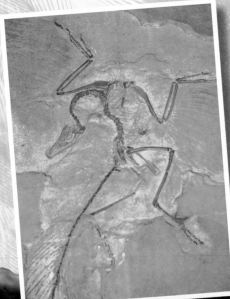

In fact, the fossil of the Archaeopteryx from this period clearly shows the link between reptiles and birds. It is well-known as one of the first 'missing links' to be found in support of evolution in the late 19th century, though it is not considered a direct ancestor of modern birds. Today, however, the two classes couldn't be more different. Reptiles are cold blooded and have scales. Birds, on the other hand, are warm blooded and have feathers.

What are they like?

Birds breathe air like us humans. They have a backbone, warm blood and two pairs of limbs. Over time the forelimbs adapted into wings for flying or swimming. The hind legs changed to allow them to walk, swim, perch, or grasp objects. You'll be surprised to know that even though birds can hear quite well, they have no external ears. They reproduce by means of one or more hard-shelled eggs, usually placed in a nest.

So how do we tell them apart?

There are thousands of bird species in the skies. So how do you identify the ones you see? In this book you will find information about what physical characteristics of a bird can help you make a positive identification, how to keep a life list of your sightings and what resources can help you identify different birds.

This book will give you information on the features of the many birds in Britain and northern Europe, and their distinguishing features. Short vignettes on the habitat, description and conservation status of the birds will further equip you with information that will help you.

Barn Owl

Tyto alba   Size: 33–39 cm

The most distinctive feature of the barn owl is the white heart-shaped face and dark eyes. When it is seen hunting in daylight, it appears low over the ground with a moth-like flight, hovering quite frequently. Barn owls hunt mainly at night in open country for rodents, frogs, birds, other small mammals and insects.

 The back of this bird is golden **buff** with pale grey and black **mottling**. The breast and feathered legs are white in colour.

 Found in a wide variety of open country including farmland, marshes, meadows and rough pasture.

Status: Widespread but declining resident over much of the region, but absent from much of N and W Scotland.

FACT When food is in short supply, the barn owl feeds its eldest and biggest chick, letting the others die.

Common Buzzard

Buteo buteo   Size: 43–53 cm

The common buzzard is a medium to large bird of prey. It can be distinguished from other hawks by its size. It has a **wingspan** of 122 to 152 cm and a body of 51 cm. Its **plumage** is a rich brown and it has lighter markings beneath. In flight, its wings have a ragged appearance as it glides at a tremendous height. It eats mainly small mammals and also **carrion**.

 This buzzard is broad-winged and is most often seen soaring on up-swept wings. This broad-winged raptor has a wide variety of plumages.

 This fierce bird of prey inhabits hills, wooded valleys and farmland with scattered woods.

Status: Absent or scarce in most of eastern England, although slowly spreading east.

FACT The buzzard makes an unmistakable 'mewing', calling frequently when it soars high in the sky.

Hen Harrier

Circus cyaneus   Size: 45–55 cm

This bird of prey is endangered in the UK. These birds fly low in search of food and hold their wings in a shallow 'V'. It is believed that the decreasing numbers of red grouse is to be blamed on the hen harrier preying upon them. Some gamekeepers prefer to eliminate this competition, thereby threatening the bird's survival in several areas.

 Males are a pale grey above and white below, though the upper breast is grey. The grey wings are tipped in black. The females are brown with buff underparts.

 They are found on the upland heather moorlands of Wales, northern England, Northern Ireland and Scotland.

Status: The population of hen harriers is alarmingly low in the UK, with local and regional **extinctions** in many areas.

FACT The brown female and juvenile hen harriers have white upper tail coverts, thus often being called 'ringtails'.

Common Kestrel

Falco tinnunculus   Size: 32–39 cm

The kestrel is a common bird of prey seen during the day. Its keen sight helps it to hunt and it is able to stay still even in strong winds. After it has spotted its prey it makes a short steep dive to catch it. This bird is capable of adapting to most conditions and can survive in the centre of urban settlements. In Britain, it is called simply the kestrel.

 The bird has light brown plumage. The male has a bluish-grey rump and tail, which are unbarred, whereas the female has dark bars on the brownish-red rump.

 The kestrel is found in a wide variety of habitats, from moor and heath, to farmland and urban areas.

Status: Habitat degradation has recently caused a decline in the number of kestrels in the region.

FACT Kestrels often do not build nests, preferring sites such as church towers, old windmills and hollow trees.

Marsh Harrier

Circus aeruginosus   Size: 42–56 cm

The marsh harrier has a larger size and build than the other harriers. It has a long tail and a lighter flight. While flying, it tends to hold its wings in a shallow 'V' shape. Habitat destruction, persecution, and other reasons led to an alarming decrease in the numbers of this bird. However, recent years have seen a marked growth in its population.

 The male is reddish-brown with yellowish streaks prominent on the breast. Its head and shoulders are pale yellowish-grey.

 Mainly found in eastern and south-east England, with some in the north-west, south-west and Scotland.

Status: Although the bird population is rising in the UK, it has a historical record of showing a decline in numbers.

FACT Although the birds generally nest in reedbeds, they have now also taken to nesting in cereal crops like barley.

Merlin

Falco columbarius   Size: 24–33 cm

The merlin is the smallest bird of prey in the UK. It hovers and hangs in the air trying to find food. The bird often enters into competition with other birds of prey when hunting. During the breeding season the birds behave ferociously, attacking much bigger birds if they venture too close. Most merlins are **migratory** and prefer to winter in warmer regions.

 The merlin is more heavily built than other falcons. The back of the male merlin is blue-grey. The underparts are buff and heavily streaked with black.

 The UK breeding population is thinly scattered across upland moorland from south-west England, north to Shetland.

Status: The numbers of the bird are just about recovering from a population crash in the late 20th century.

FACT Merlins are occasionally trained by falconers for hunting smaller birds but this is not a common practice nowadays.

Peregrine

Falco peregrinus   Size: 34–58 cm

The peregrine falcon is highly valued by falconers because of its skilful flying. It can dive from great heights at high speed and even fly upside down. It was used in Word War II to intercept homing pigeons. Although the survival of this bird was **threatened** due to the use of pesticides such as **DDT**, the population has now recovered due to conservation efforts.

 The bird has long and broad pointed wings. The tail is short and rounded. The upperparts are blue-grey. The top of the head is blackish with a prominent black 'moustache'.

 Found along rocky seacliffs and the uplands of the UK as both are good places in the breeding season.

Status: The bird is not threatened and the population is recovering having previously dipped.

 FACT To improve air-traffic safety at airports, peregrines are used to scare away other birds to reduce the risk of bird strikes.

Red Kite

Milvus milvus   Size: 60–66 cm

This bird of prey appears magnificent in flight with its **rufous** body and its striking wings. Its wingspan is about 1.6 metres and it looks elegant and graceful as it soars. Although hunted and persecuted to near extinction, its numbers have now recovered after efforts were made to conserve the species. Apart from its impressive wings, the bird has a forked tail.

 The colour of the body, upper tail and wing coverts are reddish-brown. The white in the flight feathers contrasts with the black wing tips.

 Once confined to Wales, reintroduction schemes have brought them back to many parts of England and Scotland.

Status: The bird has experienced severe decline in its numbers in the past and conservation efforts are in place.

FACT The bird is not above performing aerial piracy and sometimes snatches food from other birds, called 'kleptoparasitism'!

Common Blackbird

Turdus merula   Size: 24–25 cm

The blackbird is one of the most common garden birds in the UK. The male of the species lives up to its name with its black colour. The bright orange-yellow beak and eye-ring make the bird even more striking. Its mellow song makes the bird even more of a favourite. This bird lives on a diet of insects, worms and berries. The hardy bird can live in any type of habitat.

 Black plumage and yellow bill identify the adult male. The female is more variable, with brown plumage and mottled breast and brown bill.

 It inhabits a wide variety of habitats and is found almost everywhere except barren uplands; familiar in gardens and parks.

Status: The species is not threatened and has been listed as a species of **least concern**.

 FACT The male blackbirds might live up to their name but confusingly, the females are actually brown, often with spots.

Eurasian Golden Plover

Pluvialis apricaria   Size: 24–25 cm

Flocks of this largish plover can be seen in winter, flying in tight formations. The bird nests on the ground in open areas in their breeding habitat, which is in the northernmost parts of Europe and western parts of Asia. Due to habitat destruction places such as Poland see the plover only as a migratory species now and breeding does not occur here any more.

 The **crown**, back and wings of the golden plover are spotted with gold and black. The black face and neck is bordered with white. The rest of the bird is black.

 It inhabits upland moorlands in the Uplands and Highlands of Scotland, the Western and Northern Isles District.

Status: Widespread but declining resident over much of the region, but absent from much of N and W Scotland.

FACT In winter the bird loses its black plumage which is replaced by buff and white. It then has a yellowish face and breast.

Great Spotted Woodpecker

Dendrocopos major   Size: 23–26 cm

Although this woodpecker is a common bird, it is very difficult to spot as it will go to great lengths to avoid observation. The bird is mainly seen clinging to the trunk or branches of a tree in search of food. It prises off fragments from the bark and extracts food from the crevices with its sticky tongue.

 The bird has striking black and white plumage. There is an oval-shaped white patch on each wing and under the tail there is a red patch.

 Common in England and Wales. Only a handful of pairs nest in Ireland, but numbers are increasing.

Status: The bird is common and is not threatened. As a matter of fact, it is listed as a species of least concern.

FACT These birds create a mechanical drumming sound produced by the repeated blows of the bird's strong bill upon a tree.

Green Woodpecker

Picus viridis   Size: 30–36 cm

The green woodpecker is the largest of the woodpeckers that breed in Britain. Unlike other species of the bird, this one spends most of its time on the ground, foraging for its favourite food, ants. To help it in its collection of ants, the bird has a tongue that wraps to the back of its head. Unlike other woodpeckers, the green woodpecker does not often 'drum' on trees.

 The bird is green above and pale yellowish-green below. The rump is yellow and the crown and **nape** is red.

 A lowland species that breeds in open **deciduous** woodland, parks, orchards and farmland in England, Wales and Scotland, but is not found in Ireland.

Status: The bird is common and not threatened. It is listed as a species of least concern.

FACT Green woodpeckers have a laughing 'yaffle' call. Among its many English folk names is 'yaffle' and 'laughing betsy'.

Grey Wagtail

Motacilla cinerea　　　　Size: 18–20 cm

Grey wagtails are found walking solo or in pairs on open marshy ground or meadows where they capture and eat insects. They have a low **undulating** flight. The bird finds areas close to fast-running upland streams most favourable. This bird has graceful and delicate movements. They get their name from the fact that they frequently wag their tail and fly low.

 The upperparts of the bird are grey and it has a yellow vent which contrasts with its whitish underparts. The male has a white throat and black moustache.

 Found over most of the UK, with the exception of the northern and western isles of Scotland.

Status: Although this species is not threatened, a recent decline in population is a cause of worry.

FACT To mark its territory the bird wags its tail that is highlighted by the yellow undertail coverts and white outer tail feathers.

Eurasian Jay

Garrulus glandarius　　　　Size: 34 cm

The jay is a shy bird. While this bird is difficult to spot in person, its screaming call is easier to hear and is usually uttered when it is on the move. Even then however, it is difficult to distinguish this bird as it is an expert in mimicry and can sound like a different species altogether. It uses this skill to mimic the call of the birds it is attacking at times.

 The true colours can only be discerned when seen well. Usually only a flash of their bright white rump and black tail is visible when they are flying.

 Found across most of the UK, except northern Scotland; live in both deciduous and coniferous woodland.

Status: This bird is not threatened and is quite common. It has been listed as a species of least concern.

FACT Jays are famed for their habit of hoarding acorns and have been observed burying them in autumn to be retrieved in winter.

Lesser Spotted Woodpecker

Dendrocopos minor   Size: 15 cm

The lesser spotted woodpecker has the same habits as the greater spotted woodpecker. It is a stumpy bird seen pecking at rotten tree bark in search of grubs. The bird can usually be located by its quiet call and drumming. It has a jerky undulating flight pattern. Its note is a repeated 'keek' – loud for so small a bird.

 The bird has broad bars on the wings and narrower bars across the lower back. The male has a crimson crown and a black nape and back.

 In the UK, it is mainly limited to the south with the highest density of population occurring in the south-east of England.

Status: The conservation status of this bird in the UK is not very favourable and their population has declined seriously.

 FACT This bird drums on trees with rapid vibrations – like the greater spotted woodpecker – but with less resonance.

European Robin

Erithacus rubecula   Size: 12.5–14 cm

In the UK, this bird is also known as ruddock, robinet, or simply robin. It is a frequent visitor to gardens and often seen near a gardener digging up the soil. The bird also follows foraging animals like the wild boar in hopes of being led to food as the animal digs the soil. The male robin is very territorial and a ferocious fighter.

 The bird has an orange-red breast and face. Its wings and back are olive-brown whereas its underparts are white or light brown with a blue-grey fringe.

 The robin is found everywhere across the UK, in woodlands, hedgerows, parks and gardens.

Status: The bird is common and faces no threat. This bird is listed as a species of least concern.

FACT In the 1960s, in a much publicised vote in the Parliament, the robin was adopted as the national bird of the UK.

Bearded Tit

Panurus biarmicus   Size: 16.5 cm

The bearded tit is a brown, long-tailed bird and can usually be spotted streaking across the top of a reedbed. This bird is highly sociable and quite noisy. The first clue to its presence is usually the 'ping' call it makes. Groups of them can be seen exploding occasionally from reedbeds as they relocate to better feeding areas in the vicinity.

 The bird is long tailed and has a general tawny colouring. The male has a blue-grey head with a black moustache and a distinctive loud ping call.

 This bird is restricted to large reedbeds in eastern and southern England; a minority winter in southern Europe.

Status: Local and largely resident, with periodic movements to and from mainland Europe (mainly Holland).

FACT

Contrary to its name, the bearded tit actually has a black moustache, not a beard. This is its distinguishing mark.

Blue Tit

Parus caeruleus   Size: 12 cm

The colourful blue, yellow, white and green of the blue tit makes it one of the most attractive garden birds in Britain. This common woodland and garden bird can be seen almost all the year round. It gives perky acrobatic performances when feeding. In birdhouses and cages it swings beneath the holder, calling 'tee, tee, tee' or a scolding 'churr'.

 This bird is small and colourful, with the combination of blue and yellow making it easily identifiable. It is one of the most colourful garden visitors.

 The bird is found in the deciduous and mixed woodlands, gardens, parks and **hedgerows** in temperate Europe.

Status: Widely and abundantly distributed over most of Britain, it is listed as a species of least concern.

FACT

Blue tits frequently, especially in winter, tear open the foil tops of milk bottles, drinking the top layer of milk.

Bullfinch

Pyrrhula pyrrhula   Size: 15 cm

The male is unmistakable with his bright pinkish-red breast and cheeks, grey back, black cap and tail, and bright white rump. The flash of the rump in flight and the sad call note are usually the first signs of a bullfinch being present. It feeds voraciously on the buds of various trees in spring and was once considered a pest of fruit crops.

 The bird is plump and bull-necked. The male is red, black, grey and white with distinctive plumage. The female has a similar pattern, but duller breast colour.

 This species of bird lives on the edges of woodlands and is found in hedgerows, orchards and large gardens.

Status: This species is a widespread but declining resident. It is listed as a species of least concern.

FACT During the nesting season the bullfinch is a woodland bird; the only sign of its presence is a soft piping or a fleeting vision.

Carrion Crow

Corvus corone   Size: 48–52 cm

The all-black carrion crow is one of the cleverest, most adaptable of our birds. It is generally quite fearless, even though it is a little wary of man. The bird gets its name from the fact that it scavenges the carcasses of dead animals. The crow likes to position itself on the top branches of isolated trees from where it can observe all that is happening in its surroundings.

 The plumage of this all-black crow has a greenish or purplish sheen. It has a stout beak which makes it look short. The legs and feet are also black.

 The carrion crow is found all over the United Kingdom except in northern and western Scotland and Northern Ireland.

Status: The crow is common in Britain and is not considered threatened.

FACT The carrion crow is a very crafty egg thief and even steals the chicks of other birds and eat grubs and insects.

Chaffinch

Fringilla coelebs　　　　Size: 14–16 cm

The chaffinch (also called by a wide variety of other names) is one of the most common birds in the UK. It was introduced in Britain in the 18th and 19th centuries from overseas territories. The bird blends in with the surroundings during feeding because of its plumage and is most noticeable in flight. It is famous for its various calls and loud songs.

 It has double white bars on its wings, white tail edges and a greenish rump. During breeding season, the male has reddish underparts and a blue-grey cap.

 It is found around the UK in woodlands, hedgerows, fields, parks and gardens – in fact almost anywhere!

Status: It is a common bird and is not threatened. It has been classified as a species of least concern.

 FACT The chaffinch can only learn to sing properly if it is exposed to the adult male's song during a particular period.

Common Crossbill

Loxia curvirostra　　　　Size: 15–17 cm

The crossbill flies at tree-top height in large family flocks. It is a noisy species. The bird has a bill that is crossed at the tip, which is what earned the bird its name in the first place. The crossbill is often referred to as the 'parrot of the northern woods'. It frequently calls out when in flight. It feeds on conifer cones, particularly the spruce, Douglas-fir and pine species.

 The adult male has a distinctive brick-red plumage and the female is greyish with greenish-yellow chest and rump. The tail is forked.

 This bird has established breeding areas in the Scottish Highlands, the north Norfolk coast, and Breckland.

Status: It is a common bird and is not threatened. It has been listed as a species of least concern.

FACT The crossed bill of the bird enables it to extract seeds from pine cones, which are its principle food.

Goldcrest

Regulus regulus Size: 8.5–9.5 cm

The goldcrest is the smallest European songbird, weighing only about 5 grams. The bird is closely associated with coniferous forests. Currently the goldcrest population in the UK is quite healthy owing to mild winters but a harsh cold season could threaten their survival. The goldcrest's high call ends in a flourish with the pitch slightly descending.

 The tiny bird has dull greenish upperparts and buff or white underparts. There are two white wingbars and an orange or yellow **crest**.

 It is found all over the UK, almost wherever there are trees and bushes, especially conifers.

Status: The bird is common and is not threatened. It is listed as a species of least concern.

 FACT Goldcrests build their well-hidden nests on conifers. As the nest gets higher, it narrows with an opening at the top.

Hawfinch

Coccothraustes coccothraustes Size: 16.5–18 cm

This bird is very shy and is rarely seen. It is extremely cautious and disappears when it sees humans approaching, even at a distance. Its erratic behaviour in regard to habitat and nesting makes it difficult to ascertain its numbers. The bird has an elaborate courtship ritual where the male shows off its **iridescent** purple and green flight feathers.

 The bird seems very short-tailed in flight. The upper parts of the bird are dark brown and the underparts are orange. It has a black eye-stripe and bib.

 Hawfinches are now mostly restricted to England in the UK and a few other areas like western England.

Status: The population of this bird has seriously declined in the UK, as breeding areas have contracted.

 FACT Hawfinches have a huge strong bill that is capable of cracking open cherry stones, and a big head to match.

Great Cormorant

Phalacrocorax carbo   Size: 70–102 cm

With its long neck, the cormorant looks quite primitive, some might even call it reptilian. It is commonly seen trying to dry its wings by holding them out. The cormorant is a fantastic fisher and many fishermen find it difficult to compete with. Although it can dive to great depths it often feeds at the surface. The bird is regarded as greedy and sinister by some though.

 The bird has black plumage, a fairly long tail and yellow throat-patch. During the breeding season, the adults develop white thigh patches.

 The bird is found around the UK coastline on rocky shores, coastal lagoons and estuaries.

Status: It is a common bird and is not threatened. It has been listed as a species of least concern.

FACT In countries like China and Japan fishermen use cormorants on leashes to catch fish, known as ukai in Japan.

European Shag

Phalacrocorax aristotelis   Size: 68–78 cm

The European shag or common shag is a type of cormorant. Although the shag looks very much like the cormorant, it is smaller and slimmer with a steeper forehead. It dives deep for its food and can remain underwater for 25 to 40 seconds. It finds its prey on the sea bottom and comes up with it. The sand eel is its common prey.

 This bird has a long tail and a yellow throat-patch. In the breeding season a crest appears in adults. The dark plumage has a metallic green tint.

 In the UK it breeds on coastal sites, mainly in the north and west. Half its population is found at less than 10 sites.

Status: The bird is threatened as it breeds in a small number of areas. However it is still listed as a species of least concern.

FACT The name 'shag' originates from the Old Norse word 'skegg' which means beard and refers to the crest.

Common Shelduck

Tadorna tadorna   Size: 61 cm

The common shelduck is a widespread and common duck. The shelduck is mainly white and flies with heavy slow-beating wings. The young of these birds form large **crèches** at the time of the moulting season. These nurseries can be quite large with very few adults in attendance. If they are frightened or wounded, these birds have a tendency to dive underwater.

 The bird has a red bill and the adult male develops a swollen red bill knob in the breeding season. The head and neck is blackish-green.

 In the UK, shelducks are found mainly in coastal areas, although they can also be found around inland waters.

Status: The bird has a small breeding population. However, it has been listed as a species of least concern.

FACT Shelducks are unable to fly for four weeks at the time of moulting as they need to renew their tail and wing feathers.

Herring Gull

Larus argentatus   Size: 66 cm

The herring gull is a large gull and is the most abundant and best known of all gulls along the shores of Asia, western Europe, and North America. This bird is a large, noisy gull and found throughout the year around British coasts and inland around rubbish tips, fields, large reservoirs and lakes, especially during winter. The loud laughing call is well-known.

 The adult has a light grey back, white under parts, and black wing tips. Its legs are pink. Its heavy, slightly hooked bill is marked with a red spot.

 It breeds across North America, Europe and Asia. Some herring gulls migrate further south in winter.

Status: Herring gulls are widespread and can easily be seen at virtually any seaside town in the breeding season.

FACT Herring gulls are abundant around inland garbage dumps, and some have even adapted to life in inland cities.

Eurasian Bittern

Botaurus stellaris   Size: 76 cm

The bittern is a kind of wading bird that usually frequents reedbeds and similar marshy areas. It feeds on small amphibians, reptiles, insects, and fish. This bird is more likely to be heard than seen. The males have a loud booming call during the breeding season that can be heard from over two kilometres away! The bird is highly secretive and its mottled plumage helps it stay hidden.

 This is a thick-necked, medium-sized, golden brown bird. The bird is very shy and secretive and it blends well into its reedy home.

 Found in wetlands and marshes with extensive reedbeds and other wet areas, including ponds, ditches, and rice fields.

Status: Very scarce and local resident with the main breeding strongholds in Lancashire and East Anglia.

FACT When the bittern is startled, it stands with its bill pointing upwards and neck stretched out vertically.

Grey Heron

Ardea cinerea   Size: 90–100 cm

The grey heron is the largest heron in Europe. While looking for food the bird stands with its neck stretched out or it may hunch with its neck near its chest. In slow flight, the bird holds its head in a retracted S-shape. The bird **stalks** its prey standing motionless for hours in the water or wading slowly. It feeds in shallow water, catching fish, frogs, and insects with its long bill.

 The plumage is mainly grey above and off-white below. White-headed adults have a broad black **supercilium** and a slender crest. The wings are rounded.

 It is found all over the UK in wetland marshes, gravel pits, reservoirs, lakes, rivers and estuaries.

Status: It is very widely distributed, is quite common and not threatened. It has been listed as a species of least concern.

FACT During the breeding season the heron's bill and legs change colour to deep orange and the bird dances with its wings open.

Northern Lapwing

Vanellus vanellus Size: 28–31 cm

The northern lapwing, also known as the peewit, green plover or just lapwing, is a bird in the plover family. It is a wader which breeds on cultivated land and other short vegetation habitats. This is a vocal bird in the breeding season, and calls constantly. Like the golden plovers, this species prefers to feed **nocturnally** when there are moonlit nights.

 It has rounded wings and a crest. It is the shortest-legged of the lapwings. It is mainly black and white, but the back is tinted green.

 It is common through temperate Eurasia but is highly migratory over most of its extensive range.

Status: This species has been adversely affected by intensive agricultural techniques but is listed as a species of least concern.

 FACT The name lapwing has been attributed to the 'lapping' sound its wings make in flight.

Oystercatcher

Haematopus ostralegus Size: 40–48 cm

The Eurasian oystercatcher, also known as the common pied oystercatcher, or just oystercatcher, is a wader in the oystercatcher bird family. This is a large, obvious and noisy plover-like bird. It is the most widespread of the oystercatchers. This particular oystercatcher is the national bird of the Faroe Islands, where it is called tjaldur.

 It is a black and white bird with red legs and strong broad red bill used for smashing or prising open molluscs or for finding earthworms.

 The bird breeds mainly in northern Europe, but in winters, can be found in north Africa and southern Europe.

Status: The Eurasian oystercatcher is found in very large numbers and is listed as a species of least concern.

 FACT Despite their name, oysters do not form a large part of the oystercatcher's diet.

Black-tailed Godwit

Limosa limosa   Size: 33–39 cm

The black-tailed godwit is a large wading bird with a very long straight bill and long legs. This bird has suffered a large population decline in the past and is now a rare breeder. It feeds largely in grasslands, moving to muddy estuaries after breeding and for winter. For many years the bird was a rarity, but has become much more abundant in recent years as its numbers have recovered due to conservation efforts.

 The male has a bright orange breast, neck and head. The legs are dark grey, brown or black.

 Godwits breed in the river valley fens, floods at the edges of large lakes, damp steppes, raised bogs and moorlands.

Status: Rare breeder; this species is classified as near threatened due to a 25% decline in numbers in the past 15 years.

FACT During the breeding season, the bill of the godwit has a yellowish or orange-pink base and a dark tip.

Eurasian Curlew

Numenius arquata   Size: 50–57 cm

The curlew is the largest European shorebird. This wading bird's beautiful trills haunt the estuaries, marshes and shores where it is found. Because of habitat loss (due to the growth of agriculture which encroaches on its territory) there has been a decline in the population of this bird. It is unique among curlews as it shows a prominent white back and rump in flight.

 The curlew has streaked plumage and is generally greyish-brown with a white back. It has brown underparts and long legs. The bill is long and sickle-shaped.

 The bird is found around the UK coastline, northern Wales, the southern uplands and Scottish highlands.

Status: The status of the bird is near threatened. Though a rather common bird, its numbers are declining.

FACT The bird gets its name from its most familiar call which is a loud 'curloo-oo'. It is called a 'whaup' in Scotland.

Lesser Black-backed Gull

Larus fuscus   Size: 52–64 cm

The lesser black-backed gull is a large gull. It is an **omnivore** like most Larus gulls, and will eat fish, insects, **crustaceans**, worms, starfish, molluscs, seeds, berries, small mammals, eggs, small birds, chicks, scraps and even carrion. It is similar in size to the herring gull or just slightly smaller. More than half the UK population is found at fewer than ten sites.

 This bird has a slim build and yellow legs. The adults have black or dark grey wings and back. The bill is yellow with a red spot.

 The bird breeds in the Atlantic coasts of Europe. It is migratory, wintering from the British Isles south to West Africa.

Status: Their world population is found entirely in Europe; listed as a species of least concern.

FACT The lesser black-backed gull has a 'laughing' cry like that of the herring gull but with a markedly deeper pitch.

Purple Heron

Ardea purpurea   Size: 80–90 cm

The purple heron is a wading bird in the heron family. The bird feeds in shallow water. It spears fish, frogs, insects, small mammals, reptiles and small birds with its beak and will either wait motionless for prey in one spot, or slowly stalk its victims. It is a shy and solitary hunter, and appears to hunt mostly at night, often continuing into the early morning.

 It has dark reddish-brown plumage, and adults develop darker grey backs. It has a narrow yellow bill, which is brighter in breeding adults.

 The bird breeds in colonies in reed beds or close to extensive wetlands in Africa, Europe, and Asia.

Status: This bird has been listed as a species of least concern.

FACT The long neck of the purple heron looks particularly snake-like, with more of an S-shape in flight.

Barnacle Goose

Branta leucopsis   Size: 60–70 cm

The barnacle goose is a medium-sized bird that makes a barking or yapping sound. It nests high on mountain cliffs. It does not feed its young, but encourages the goslings to jump off the cliff edge as they develop the wings to fly. Some are protected by their soft down from serious injury but significant numbers die or are captured by predators as a result.

 The bird has a white face but the head, neck and upper breast are black. The belly is white. The back and wings have black and white barring.

 The bird is found largely on the Solway Firth in England and Scotland and on Islay, Scotland.

Status: The conservation of this bird is a concern. However, it is still listed as a species of least concern.

FACT A legend had it that the geese developed underwater in the form of barnacles. This is where they get their name from.

Egyptian Goose

Alopochen aegyptiacus   Size: 63–73 cm

The Egyptian goose was introduced in Britain as ornamental wildfowl in the 18th century. Now there is a considerable feral population. In 2009 the bird was officially declared to be a pest in the UK as they are thought to pose a threat either to native wildlife, public health or public safety. It is a largely land-based species and perches readily on trees and buildings.

 The colour of the bird can vary from grey-brown to red-brown. It has dark brown eye-patches. The beak and legs are pink.

 The bird is found mainly in eastern England. The north Norfolk coast holds the highest numbers.

Status: The bird is common and not threatened. It has been listed as a species of least concern.

FACT Egyptian geese were considered to be sacred by the Ancient Egyptians and were often represented in their artworks.

Great Crested Grebe

Podiceps cristatus Size: 46–51 cm

This waterbird was once hunted almost to extinction as its ornate head plumes were much in demand to adorn the hats of ladies. It is an excellent swimmer and diver, and dives underwater for food as well as to escape danger. The great crested grebe also has an elaborate courtship display during which the bird rises out of the water and shakes its head.

 The bird has a slender outline, long neck and bill and reddish-orange, black-tipped head plumes in summer. Its legs are set back on its body.

 It is found in lowland lakes, gravel pits, reservoirs and rivers. In winters it is also found along the coasts.

Status: The bird is common and not threatened. It has been listed as a species of least concern.

FACT The heads of very young great crested grebes are striped in white and black, resembling the markings of zebras.

Common Kingfisher

Alcedo atthis Size: 16 cm

If you see streaks of bright blue and orange flitting over slow-moving or still water, they probably belongs to the kingfisher. Its iridescent plumage makes it very easily recognisable. This bird was once persecuted as its feathers were in demand to decorate ladies' hats. The low-flying bird hunts fish from its perches. It is also known as the Eurasian kingfisher.

 The upperparts are coloured bright blue, while the underparts are a rich chestnut-red. In females, the base of the bill is red and in males it is black.

 It is widespread, especially in central and southern England, becoming less common further north.

Status: Habitat degradation is a cause of worry. They are listed as a species of least concern.

FACT Kingfishers are very territorial and if a bird encroaches upon another's territory, a fight may follow.

White-tailed Eagle

Haliaeetus albicilla   Size: 69–92 cm

The white-tailed eagle is a large bird of prey. It was hunted illegally and was extinct in the UK before being reintroduced. This bird is known to return to its nests to reuse them. There are records of trees collapsing under the weight of their massive nests. In Iceland there is record of a site where white-tailed eagles have been breeding for the past 150 years.

 The adult is typically brown with paler head and neck, broad wings, and a thick yellow beak. It has a white tail and its legs are yellow.

 This large eagle breeds in northern Europe and northern Asia with the largest population found in Norway.

Status: Became extinct in most of Europe, but has recovered after being reintroduced. It is a species of least concern.

FACT In the Shetland Isles, fishermen used to smear eagle fat on their bait to increase their catch.

Gyrfalcon

Falco rusticolus   Size: 48–61 cm

The gyrfalcon, also spelled gerfalcon, is the largest of all falcon species. The bird's common name comes from the French 'gerfaucon', and in medieval Latin is 'gyrofalco'. It feeds only on birds and mammals. It hunts its prey by chasing it from the air and pouncing on it. Whether it is a bird or a small mammal, the prey is killed on the ground.

 They have pointed wings, but are stockier, broader-winged, and longer-tailed than the peregrine falcon.

 The gyrfalcon is a tundra and mountain bird and breeds in Arctic coasts and islands of North America, Europe and Asia.

Status: It is classified as a species of least concern. However, commercial markets in falconry may pose a threat.

FACT The male gyrfalcon is called a gyrkin in falconry and is the largest of all falcons.

European Bee-eater

Merops apiaster   Size: 27–29 cm

The European bee-eater nests in colonies, burrowing into sandy banks. As the name suggests, the bee-eater eats insects, especially bees, wasps and hornets that are caught in the air by sorties from an open perch. It is one of the few European species in which the young are fed, by additional 'helpers', not just the parents.

 This bird is a richly-coloured, slender bird. It has brown and yellow upper parts, while the wings are green and the beak is black.

 It breeds in holes in sandpits, riverbanks and quarries in Europe and in parts of north Africa and western Asia.

Status: The bird is common and not threatened. It has been identified as a species of least concern.

FACT Before eating its meal, a European bee-eater removes the sting by repeatedly hitting the insect on a hard surface.

Black Woodpecker

Dryocopus martius   Size: 45–47 cm

The black woodpecker is a large woodpecker, with a 64–78 cm wingspan. It lives in mature forests across the northern Palearctic. It is the sole representative of its genus in that region. Its range is expanding in Eurasia. It does not migrate. It has a large, dagger-shaped bill, broad at the base and tapering to a sharp, chisel tip.

 The plumage of this crow-sized woodpecker is entirely black apart from a red crown. It has a very long beak of 6 cm – almost 60% of its skull length.

 It is not uncommon locally from Spain, France and the Low Countries in the west, to Italy and Greece to the south.

Status: The population is large and appears to be increasing. Hence, it is listed as a species of least concern.

FACT The black woodpecker's hearing is so good, it can hear carpenter ants crawling inside a tree trunk.

Whinchat

Saxicola rubetra   Size: 12.5 cm

The whinchat is a small European bird. Its scientific name means 'reddish rock-dweller', in reference to its habitat and overall colouration. The whinchat is similar in size to its relative the European robin. It hops or runs on the ground and often perches on top of low bushes. The bird likes to perch on elevated spots from where it can dart to catch flying insects.

 The bird has brownish upperparts, a yellowish rump, a buff throat and breast, a whitish belly, and a blackish tail.

 The bird breeds in upland areas of northern and western Britain with a few in Ireland. It winters in central and southern Africa.

Status: The whinchat is not uncommon across its wide range and is thus listed as a species of least concern.

FACT In summer, on the moors, whinchats can be heard singing their rasping song from a low perch.

Meadow Pipit

Anthus pratensis   Size: 12.5–14.0 cm

The meadow pipit, or titlark, is a small bird that is widespread and often abundant. It is the most common songbird in upland areas and its high, piping call is a familiar sound. It becomes very sociable in winter and gathers in small flocks. The flocks perch hidden in the vegetation until they are disturbed, when they suddenly fly up en masse.

 It is an undistinguished looking species, brown above and buff below, with darker streaking on most of its plumage. It has pale pink legs and a thin bill.

 This bird breeds in much of the northern half of Europe and Asia. In winter it moves south, to more lowland areas.

Status: Despite a recent decline in the breeding population, it is still classified as a species of least concern.

FACT During courtship the male flies straight up in the air, then it sings, shortly followed by a direct drop to the ground.

Hooded Crow

Corvus cornix   Size: 48–52 cm

The hooded crow (sometimes called hoodiecrow) is a Eurasian bird species in the crow genus. The hooded crow is closely related to the carrion crow, and until recently was regarded as the same species. Like carrion crows, the hoodie also feeds on dead animals. It can be more sociable in feeding habits and groups of them may be seen together in fields.

 It is an ashy grey bird with black head, throat, wings, tail and thigh feathers, as well as a black bill, eyes and feet.

 Found across northern, eastern and southeastern Europe, and the Middle East. Other, closely allied forms inhabit southern Europe and western Asia.

Status: There has been no significant decline in their populations and they are listed as a species of least concern.

FACT The hooded crow was one of the species originally described by Linnaeus in his 18th-century work *Systema Naturae.*

Fieldfare

Perisoreus infaustus   Size: 22–27 cm

The fieldfare is a member of the thrush family. It stands very upright and moves forward with purposeful hops. It is a very social bird, spending the winter in flocks of anything from a dozen or two to several hundred strong. It usually nests in colonies of 5–20 pairs. It has been shown that pairs that nest in colonies are more successful as they are not hunted.

 It has a plain brown back, white underwings, and grey rump and rear head. The breast has a reddish wash, and the underparts are white.

 It breeds in woodland and scrub in northern Europe and Asia. It is found in fields, open country and hedgerows.

Status: The fieldfare has an extensive range and a large population and is listed as a species of least concern.

FACT Its English name dates back the eleventh century and seems to derive from the Anglo-Saxon word 'feldefare'.

Common Redpoll

Carduelis flammea   Size: 12–14 cm

The common redpoll is a species in the finch family. This bird is remarkably resistant to cold temperatures and winter movements are mainly driven by the availability of food. Busy and acrobatic, this birds **forages** in flocks along hedgerows. It can feed at the very tips of small branches, hanging upside-down, and using its feet to hold food items.

 The male is heavily streaked and has a small, red crown and a pink breast. It also shows two white lines on the wings when they are folded.

 It breeds across the northern parts of North America and Eurasia, in habitats with thickets or shrubs.

Status: The habitats of the redpolls are not subject to degradation. They have been classified as of least concern.

 FACT Redpolls have throat pouches for temporarily storing seeds. They fill the pouch with seeds and swallow them later.

European Greenfinch

Carduelis chloris   Size: 14–16 cm

The European greenfinch is a small passerine bird in the finch family. It will eat seeds from conifer cones and grasses, and also insects, small fruits (mainly for their seeds) and berries. It travels in small groups looking for seeds and forms large roosting flocks at night in winter. The Greenfinch has become a common feeder in gardens.

 The bird has an olive green body with bright yellow and black feathers on the wings. The tail is also black and yellow. The bill is ivory and legs pale pink.

 This bird is widespread throughout grasslands, wastelands, and heathlands in Europe, Africa and Asia.

Status: It is not listed as threatened or endangered but classified as a species of least concern.

 FACT The thick bill of the European greenfinch is well-adapted to eating the seeds of conifers.

Atlantic Puffin

Fratercula arctica   Size: 28–34 cm

The Atlantic puffin is a seabird species in the auk family. It feeds primarily by diving for fish, but also eats other sea creatures, such as squid and crustaceans. Its most obvious characteristic is its brightly coloured beak during the breeding seasons. The characteristic bright orange bill plates grow before the breeding season and are shed after breeding.

 This bird is mainly black above and white below, with grey to white cheeks and red-orange legs. The bill is large and triangular.

 This species breeds on the coasts of northern Europe, the Faroe Islands, Iceland and eastern North America.

Status: These birds have been increasing in population by about 10% per year and have been listed as of least concern.

FACT The curious appearance of the bird has given rise to nicknames such as "clown of the ocean" and "sea parrot".

Common Eider

Somateria mollissima   Size: 50–71 cm

The common eider, is a large sea-duck. The eider's nest is built close to the sea and is lined with the celebrated eiderdown, plucked from the female's breast. This species dives for crustaceans and molluscs, with mussels being a favoured food. The eider will eat mussels by swallowing them whole, the shells are then crushed in their stomachs and excreted.

 The common eider has a bulky shape and large wedge-shaped bill. The male has black and white plumage and a green nape.

 It is distributed over the northern coasts of Europe, North America and eastern Siberia.

Status: These birds have a healthy population and have been listed as of least concern.

FACT A colony on Farne Islands in the UK was the subject of one of the first ever bird protection laws in the year 676.

Arctic Tern

Sterna paradisaea   Size: 33–39 cm

The Arctic tern is a seabird of the tern family. The species is strongly migratory, migrating from its northern breeding grounds to the oceans around Antarctica and back each year. It lives together in groups of about 50 terns that are called colonies. Sometimes the colony will adopt different species of terns and sea gulls in their midst.

 It is mainly grey and white plumed, with a red beak and feet, white forehead, a black nape and crown, and white cheeks.

 This bird breeds colonially in Arctic and sub-Arctic regions of Europe, Asia, and North America.

Status: The species is abundant with an estimated one million individuals, so is listed as of least concern.

FACT Even though it is small, the distance that it migrates is one of the longest of any bird: 35,000 km yearly!

Common Gull

Larus canus   Size: 40–46 cm

The common gull, mew gull or sea mew is a medium-sized gull and is most likely to be mistaken for a herring gull. However, this bird is much smaller in size. It usually feeds on worms, insects, fish, carrion and rubbish. Common gulls often try to obtain their food by snatching it from other birds such as lapwings, a behaviour known as kleptoparasitism.

 This bird is grey above and white below. The legs are greenish-yellow. In winter, the head is streaked grey. The legs are greenish and beak yellow.

 The bird breeds along coasts and inland marshes in northern Asia, northern Europe and northwestern America.

Status: The common gull is not threatened at present and is listed as a species of least concern.

 FACT Its called common, not because it is abundant, but because in winter it feeds on common land, pastures.

Northern Fulmar

Fulmarus glacialis   Size: 46 cm

The northern fulmar looks superficially like a gull, but is unrelated, and is in fact a petrel. A gull-like relative of albatrosses and shearwaters, the northern fulmar is a bird of the northern oceans. When eating fish, they will dive up to several metres underwater to retrieve their prey. They make grunting and chuckling sounds while eating and guttural calls during the breeding season.

 The species is grey and white with a pale yellow, thick bill and bluish legs. It has moderately long, rounded wings, a short stout, pale bill and a short rounded tail.

 The northern fulmar lives in the North Atlantic and North Pacific region and breeds on steep sea cliffs.

Status: There is no immediate threat to this bird and it is listed as a species of least concern.

FACT The fulmar gets its name from the old Norse word meaning foul gull, a reference to its stomach oils.

Great Skua

Stercorarius skua   Size: 50–58 cm

The great skua is a large seabird in the skua family. The great skua is an aggressive pirate of the seas, deliberately harrassing birds as large as gannets to steal a free meal. It also readily kills and eats smaller birds such as puffins. This bird eats mainly fish, which it often obtains by robbing gulls, terns and even northern gannets of their catches.

 Adults are streaked greyish brown, with a black cap. Their tail is short and blunt. At a distance they look stout and dark and show white wing flashes in flight.

 The great skua breeds in Iceland, Norway, the Faroe Islands and the Scottish islands.

Status: The population of this bird has been growing rapidly causing it to be listed as a species of least concern.

FACT This Skua's call is a harsh 'hah-hah-hah-hah'; quacking and croaking noises have also been heard.

Razorbill

Alca torda   Size: 38–43 cm

The razorbill is a large auk. This bird forages for food by swimming underwater. It can stay underwater for about one minute before surfacing. It mainly eats fish, some crustaceans and marine worms. The bird catches and eats its prey underwater. The bird only comes to the shore to breed.

 The adult bird is black on its upperparts and white on the breast and belly. The thick black bill has a blunt end. The tail is pointed and long.

 This bird usually breeds on islands, rocky shores and cliffs on northern Atlantic coasts.

Status: Populations are thought to be stable or increasing and it is listed as a species of least concern.

FACT The oldest known razorbill was a female, banded in 1962 and resighted, breeding, in 2000, 38 years later.

Black-browed Albatross

Thalassarche melanophrys   Size: 80–95 cm

The black-browed albatross is the commonest albatross species. It forages for food in waters over continental shelves, which unfortunately puts it in the way of longline and trawl fisheries. This marine bird returns to land only for breeding. It is also commonly known as a mollyhawk and feeds on fish, squid, crustacea, carrion, and fishery discards.

 Its underparts are mainly white. The upperwing is dark grey. The yellow bill has a darker orange tip. The dark eye-stripe gives the bird its common name.

 The black-browed albatross is a bird of the southern oceans and breeds on various islands throughout this region.

Status: This species has been classified as endangered due to drastic reduction in its population.

FACT The bird has a salt gland above the nasal passage that excretes a solution from its nose that helps it to desalinate its body.

Ruddy Turnstone

Arenaria interpres   Size: 22–24 cm

The ruddy turnstone is a small wading bird, one of two species of turnstone in the genus Arenaria. It breeds in northern latitudes, usually no more than a few kilometres from the sea. A stocky, brightly patterned shorebird, the ruddy turnstone can be seen actively pecking, probing, and flipping over stones and other objects along rocky shores.

 The plumage is a **harlequin**-like pattern of black and white. Breeding birds have reddish-brown upper parts with black markings on them.

 It is a highly migratory bird, breeding in northern parts of Eurasia and North America and flying south to winter.

Status: Populations of this bird are relatively stable and it is classified as a species of least concern.

FACT The ruddy turnstone has a staccato, rattling call and a chattering alarm-call given in the breeding season.

White Stork

Ciconia ciconia   Size: 100–125 cm

The white stork is a large wading bird in the stork family. In mythology, this national bird of Poland and Lithuania is responsible for bringing babies to new parents. The story probably came about because these birds have a habit of nesting on buildings in urban areas, so they are often seen around human habitation.

 It is completely white except for the black wing flight feathers, and its red bill and legs.

 The bird breeds in the warmer parts of Europe (north to Estonia), northwest Africa, and southwest Asia (east to southern Kazakhstan).

Status: Listed as a species of least concern.

FACT White storks use thermal currents of hot air for long distance flight, taking great advantage of them during migrations.

Dunlin

Calidris alpina   Size: 17–21 cm

The dunlin is a small wader. The dunlin forms large flocks on coastal mudflats or sandy beaches. Large numbers of them can often be seen swirling in **synchronised** flight. Insects form the main part of the dunlin's diet in the nesting grounds. However, the bird will also eat molluscs, worms and crustaceans in the coastal areas it is found in.

 An adult dunlin has a distinctive black belly. The winter dunlin is basically grey above and white below. The legs and slightly curved bill are black.

 It is a circumpolar breeder in Arctic or subarctic regions with large populations in northern Europe and Asia.

Status: Listed as a species of least concern. Even though they are abundant, populations may be declining.

 FACT It feeds in flocks in winter, sometimes numbering thousands, roosting on nearby fields, saltmarshes and shore.

Eurasian Crane

Grus grus   Size: 100–130 cm

The common crane, also known as the Eurasian crane, is a bird of the family Gruidae, the cranes. In Great Britain the common crane became extinct in the 17th century, but a tiny population now breeds again in the Norfolk Broads and is slowly increasing. Principal foods include insects, grain, acorns, invertebrates, frogs, lizards and rodents.

 It is grey with a white facial streak and a bunch of black wing plumes. Adults have a red crown patch.

 It breeds in wetlands in northern and western Europe across Eurasia to northern Mongolia, northern China, and eastern Siberia.

Status: Listed as a species of least concern. The main threat is the loss and degradation of breeding habitat.

FACT It is a rare visitor to western North America, where birds are occasionally seen with flocks of migrating sandhill.

Canada Goose

Branta canadensis Size: 76–110 cm

The Canada goose is a widespread species. It has been introduced intentionally in many places of the world. However, it is also regarded as a pest in many places. The bird becomes very aggressive during breeding season and even attacks humans if they come too close to the brood. Like most geese, the Canada goose is naturally migratory, flying in V-shaped formation.

 The bird has a black head and neck, white cheeks and is most identifiable because of its white 'chinstrap'. It has a brown back and a tan breast.

 Although native to North America, Canada geese have reached northern Europe naturally.

Status: Canada Geese are common and increasing in numbers and are listed as a species of least concern.

FACT This bird was introduced in Britain in the 17th century to add to King James II's water fowl collection at St. James' Park.

Mute Swan

Cygnus olor Size: 125–170 cm

The mute swan is not exactly a mute bird. It is just slightly less vocal than other birds. It makes a variety of grunting, whistling and snorting noises. When the bird flies, its wings make a vibrant throbbing noise which can be heard up to 2 kilometres away! In the UK the monarch retains the right to ownership of all unmarked mute swans in open water.

 This is a large swan with totally white plumage. It has a graceful S-shaped neck and an orange bill bordered in black with a knob on the bill.

 The bird breeds across most of Europe and Asia, and (as a rare winter visitor) in the far north of Africa.

Status: The population in the UK has increased recently, perhaps due to better protection of this species.

FACT The black knob on the male swan's bill swells during the breeding season and becomes larger than the female's.

Red-necked Grebe

Podiceps grisegena   Size: 43–56 cm

The red-necked grebe is a migratory aquatic bird. The bird is a good swimmer and a swift diver. As a matter of fact, it responds to danger by diving rather than flying. The feet are positioned far back on the body, near the tail, which makes the bird ungainly on land. The red-necked grebe migrates over land strictly at night, rarely migrating over water during the day.

 This bird is dusky-grey in winter. During the breeding season, it gets the distinctive red neck plumage, black cap and contrasting pale grey face.

 It breeds in shallow freshwater lakes, and other inland bodies of water in the temperate regions of the north.

Status: There is no clear trend in population numbers and as such it is listed as a species of least concern.

 FACT The red-necked grebe swallows its own feathers in large quantities, which help in digestion.

Greylag Goose

Anser anser   Size: 74–84 cm

Greylag geese are the ancestors of almost all species of domesticated geese. The bird feeds on tubers, grass and aquatic weeds. It is a large bird which has a loud cackling call, like the domestic goose. In autumn, while migrating, it often flocks in fields, meadows and similar bare areas. The bird is valuable game during the migration period in autumn.

 The bird's plumage has subtle tinges of brown and grey. There are bars on its back, breast and neck. The bill is triangular and the legs are pink.

 The bird can be found throughout most of Europe and across southern Siberia and central Asia as far as the Pacific.

Status: Its numbers may have declined as a breeding bird, but it is still classified as a species of least concern.

FACT Austrian zoologist Konrad Lorenz first studied the phenomenon of imprinting in the greylag goose.

Watching Birds

Birds are truly beautiful, fascinating creatures and they are all around us. They are easy to find and fun to observe. Many people study and observe birds as a hobby. This is known as birdwatching and it is one of the simplest hobbies to pursue.

Equipment

The easiest part of birdwatching is getting the equipment. You only need two things: a pair of binoculars and a field guide that will describe the birds for you. The only other things you need are a keen eye and a lot of patience to sit and study the bird without disturbing it. In fact, birdwatching is one of the least expensive hobbies a person can undertake.

Identifying the birds

Watching birds is one thing, identifying them is another. You should look at five things to identify the bird: 1) the bird's silhouette; 2) its plumage and colouration; 3) its behaviour; 4) its habitat preferences; and 5) its voice.

Sometimes you need only one or two of these clues to identify a bird. As you pursue this hobby, you will be able to identify birds with greater ease and certainty.

Finding the Birds

People can birdwatch almost anywhere: in national parks, in one's own backyard, or along the shorelines. You could also go on specialised birdwatching tours. However, wherever you go, remember to tread lightly and look sharp.

Further Reading

Pocket Guide to the Birds of Britain and North-West Europe
By Chris Kightley, Steve Madge, Dave Nurney
Published: Houghton Mifflin, 1993; 5th ed.

A Field Guide to the Birds of Britain and Europe
By Roger Tory Peterson, Guy Mountfort, P.A.D. Hollum
Houghton Mifflin Harcourt, 2001; 5th edition

Birds of Britain: An Introduction to Familiar Species of England, Scotland & Wales (A Pocket Naturalist Guide)
By James Kavanagh (Author), Raymond Leung (Illustrator)
Waterford Press, 2004; 1st edition

Websites

Birds Of Britain Bird Guide
http://www.birdsofbritain.co.uk/bird-guide/index.asp

Online Identification Guide to the Birds of Britain and Europe
http://www.surfbirds.com/ukbirdid.html

British Garden Birds
http://www.garden-birds.co.uk/

RSPB Birds of Britain and Europe
http://www.rspb.org.uk/

Glossary

Buff: A brownish-yellow colour.

Carrion: dead and decaying flesh.

Circumpolar: around or near the earth's poles.

Crèche: a gathering of very young birds.

Crest: a tuft or natural growth on the top of the head of a bird.

Crown: the top of the head.

Crustaceans: small animals whose bodies are covered by a hard shell.

DDT: a powerful insecticide that is also poisonous to humans and animals.

Deciduous: trees that shed their leaves annually.

Extinct: a species that is no longer living on earth.

Forage: look for food.

Harlequin: a pattern of brightly coloured diamond shapes.

Hedgerows: a row of bushes or trees forming a hedge.

Iridescent: brilliant, lustrous, or colourful in effect or appearance.

Kleptoparasitism: the theft of food by one animal from another.

Least concern: signifies that the bird is not at risk of extinction.

Migratory: travelling from one place to another at regular times of the year.

Mottling: marked with spots or blotches of different shades or colours.

Nape: the back of the neck.

Nocturnal: a bird that hunts and moves about at night.

Omnivorous: a bird that eats anything.

Plumage: the feathery covering of a bird.

Rufous: strong yellowish-pink to moderate orange.

Stalk: to pursue or approach prey stealthily.

Supercilium: a stripe that starts above the bird's eye, to the back of the head.

Synchronised: to do something at the same time.

Threatened: signifies that the bird is at risk of extinction.

Undulating: to have a wavy form or surface.

Wingspan: the length of a bird from one wingtip to another.

Index (by page)